THE DARK SIDE OF THE PUBLISHING INDUSTRY

What Big Publishers Don't Want You to Know

Timothy Aldred

Copyright © 2012 by Timothy Aldred

(Previously published as "Why They Gagged My Daughter")

ISBN: 978-1479171118

"We are confronted primarily with a moral issue...whether all Americans are to be afforded equal rights and equal opportunities, whether we are going to treat our fellow Americans as we want to be treated." - **U.S. President John F. Kennedy, June 11, 1963.**

ACKNOWLEDGEMENTS

I want to thank my dear friend Monica Jackson for her invaluable contributions and help in the production of this book. I could not have done it without her.

INTRODUCTION

My name is Timothy Aldred and I love America. I first came to this country in the 1970's from Jamaica, and I have the deepest respect for American aspirations and ideals.

My deep love and respect extends to American business and industrial establishments. Namely the publishing industry. I have always loved books so much! Reading is a great passion of mine, and a great pastime. I believe the American publishing industry provides a marvelous service to the people of this country, offering great opportunities for both writers and readers. However, to my shocking surprise, I have discovered through experience that there is a question as to whether or not the book industry is providing these wonderful opportunities in equal measure.

The reason I am writing about the dark side of the publishing industry is because I am not gagged, and I believe people need to know about certain things that go on in the industry, so that positive change can occur in America's long and touchy history with inequality.

A Barbara Streisand lyric says that what's too painful to recall, we simply choose to forget. Or, with regard to today's racial divisions, we simply choose to ignore. I want to give the account of how I watched my child go through a devastating experience, saw her freedom stifled, and how it broke my heart. I am writing this to illustrate how and why young people's lives continue to be adversely affected by the lingering effects of these historically engrained racial divisions.

I am writing it because the truth needs to be spoken for the benefit of the whole, instead of buried to benefit a few, at the expense of the whole.

In a sense we've come to our nation's capital to cash a check. When the architects of our republic wrote the magnificent words of the Constitution and the Declaration of Independence, they were signing a promissory note to which every American was to fall heir. This note was a promise that all men, yes, black men as well as white men, would be guaranteed the "unalienable Rights" of "Life, Liberty and the pursuit of Happiness." It is obvious today that America has defaulted on this promissory note, insofar as her citizens of color are concerned. Instead of honoring this sacred obligation, America has given the Negro people a bad check, a check which has come back marked "insufficient funds."

But we refuse to believe that the bank of justice is bankrupt. We refuse to believe that there are insufficient funds in the great vaults of opportunity of this nation. And so, we've come to cash this check, a check that will give us upon demand the riches of freedom and the security of justice. **- Excerpt from "I Have a Dream" by Dr. Martin Luther King, Jr. (Speech delivered August 28, 1963)**

I was just a young lad of seventeen when these words were first spoken, but they express the reason why I am writing this book far better than I ever could. Racism is not only lingering in obscure parts of the South. It is still lingering in the very fabric of America's flag.

Let me say that I am mindful of the fact that this is a very touchy subject and is apt to strike sensitive chords in many people, for their own personal reasons. I want to ask you, the reader, no matter your race, to please have an open heart and hear me out. *Please know that to further divide is not my intention.* My intention is the exact opposite. I want to unite us, but in order to achieve this, we must get radically honest about what is really happening in our country today, and in our day-to-day lives. Healing can be difficult, but as past progress has proven, we can do it, if we abandon our judgments for a moment and hear each other out with an open mind as human beings. Please do not take anything I say personally. Yes, at times I may seem very assertive, but everything is said in the spirit of getting honest, expressing my true feelings as an American, and making real progress in our country's race relations. I hope you can understand and appreciate that.

Bear with me for a moment while I show you something. Perhaps this is a bit of American history you are not too familiar with, or, maybe some of you are, but there is a reason I am noting it here:

In 1857, the United States Supreme Court ruled that black people were property, and as such, they had no claim to freedom. They were not free to even file a lawsuit in federal court for freedom from the white people who owned them. The decision was made in the case *Dred Scott v. Sandford*. If you are not familiar with it, you can research it online. This was a decision made by the highest legal authority in the land. Dred Scott, a slave who tried to buy his freedom from his white owner Irene Emerson for $300, had to try and get his freedom through the courts. A human tried to buy his own freedom from another human for $300. And then he had to go to a court of law to seek that freedom. Does this sound ridiculous to you?

Well, 150 years later, the same thing happened to my daughter. Dred Scott was trying to claim his right to the same freedom his white slave owner enjoyed by default, and 150 years later, Nadine Aldred had to go to court to claim the exact same thing. *Freedom.*

So much has changed in America since 1857, but so very little has changed in America since 1857.

Ironically, the American book publishing industry is one of the segments of our society in which this loss of freedom is still at an all-time high, though those who have money and power, the powers-that-be, as they are called, seem to work hard to keep this hidden and suppressed. With this particular industry as the focal point for the scope of this book, I hope to fully explain and illustrate the title, THE DARK SIDE OF THE PUBLISHING INDUSTRY, and how the reasons for the legal gag of my daughter is meaningful and relevant to *every* American.

In a rare occurrence, The Wall Street Journal wrote an article in December of 2006 entitled, "Why Book Industry Sees the World Split Still by Race." It was written by Jeff Trachtenberg. It explored the racial divide that exists in the industry in a way that doesn't seem to happen too often because of the sensitive nature of the problem. Not many people want to talk about it, or even admit this imbalance still exists within many American business infrastructures. The reason for this is both complex and simple: anger + fear + shame + guilt = denial.

My daughter, Nadine, published two novels under the pseudonym *Millenia Black*. One of the books is called THE GREAT PRETENDER and the second is called THE GREAT BETRAYAL. These two books were published in 2005 and 2006 respectively, by Penguin Group U.S.A., a giant New York publishing company.

In October of 2006, in an unprecedented undertaking, my daughter had to file a lawsuit against Penguin because they refused to afford her the same freedom they give to their white authors. It got so bad that they even refused to allow her to write a story about white characters in her second book. Nadine felt wounded by this experience and decided to take a stand rather than accept this treatment as many other writers choose to do.

In 1846 when Dred Scott first filed his lawsuit, freedom was, *by law,* synonymous with white people. And you even had to go to them to try and get what they get by default. In 2006 when my daughter filed her lawsuit, the same was still true and I'll tell you why: though the laws have changed, the basic mentality has not. What mentality? The mentality that white people are superior to black people. And the lingering presence of this mentality in business practice, and in our society at large.

Based on the evidence gleaned from her case, Penguin wanted to target black readers with my daughter's work and did not want to afford her the opportunity to reach the largest possible audience. She filed the lawsuit because this is not access white authors are ever denied. They are never told that their work must reflect their own skin color. So Nadine had to file a lawsuit and sue her publisher to get them to treat her the same way, to afford her *white people* freedom. I could not help but feel extremely proud of her for the enormous courage it took to go up against one of the biggest corporations in the entire world in pursuit of justice and the preservation of freedom. I have read online on some blogs that she has even been called the Rosa Parks of the publishing industry for being so brave.

When my daughter was seven-years-old, she came home to her mother from school one day crying because she discovered for the first time that black skin was not regarded as equal to white skin. It was peculiar to her mom at the time because of how devastated the child was over it. It's like it took the wind out of her sails. She seemed to have an acute awareness of her infinite nature and free spirit, so to discover that there was a society in place that inhibited that nature because of skin, devastated her. So I think she was not wired to fall in line with the traditional acceptance of the racial divide in publishing. Most authors seem to go along with it, or try to work around it. This was not an option for someone like Nadine, who apparently had an inherent intuition for the principles of equality. My daughter does not deserve disrespect in general, and she definitely did not deserve this type of literary disrespect.

Has what happened to Nadine ever happened to a white writer? Has any white author ever been told they could not write about white characters because their book would not be published? So why the unequal treatment for my daughter? This is why I must write this book.

I have recently read about authors such as Justine Larbalestier and Jaclyn Dolamore, *white* writers who have written *black* heroines in their books. Their publisher "white-washed" the book covers by using white models, because according to Larbalestier herself in a posting on her blog, they don't believe "black" covers will sell well to the "white" marketplace these authors have automatic access to, and are being positioned for.

I ask you: Why weren't Millenia Black's book covers white-washed for the benefit of reaching the largest possible audience? THE GREAT PRETENDER has no black characters, yet it was essentially "black-washed" with the use of black models on the cover. *Why would this be done to a book that doesn't have a single black character?*

Since this all began, I've written repeatedly to various media outlets, and even to Oprah Winfrey, whose producers are so enmeshed with the publishing houses because of Oprah's Book Club that they sent my letter to Penguin Group in the heat of the lawsuit and alerted them to the fact that I was trying to call Oprah's attention to this publisher's treatment of non-white authors. In fact, as I was told, one producer's response to my daughter's case was, "Oprah won't touch this." I don't remember for sure anymore, it has been a few years now, but I believe her name was Lisa something. And it appears that most everyone in the media feels the same way she does - they won't touch this.

I continue to wonder why.

In this book, I am going to lay out the facts that were uncovered through the discovery and deposition processes of my daughter's lawsuit - information to which I was privy as the events were unfolding, though I was not a party to the case, and I have no knowledge about the details of the eventual settlement. **My daughter has nothing to do with the writing or the production of this book in any way, shape or form**. My motivation is not to disparage anyone here, but to highlight the problem so that together we can acknowledge, address, and solve it at the level where it is happening.

Americans are being stripped of equal opportunities everyday by *other Americans*, and I believe that ignorance and secrecy are perpetuating this status quo. To effect positive change, I think people need to know the truth about how the major publishing establishments view, treat, and handle authors who are not white, and how this is simply mirroring the American society at large, a situation that needs to change once and for all, one individual at a time. I have witnessed a very stringent mindset of white as having the majority value, and non-whites as having the minority value. This is about value and worth, not population. People need to know about the everyday business practices that are being carried out even on this very day in 2010, which is robbing non-white writers of the same level of opportunity their white counterparts have by default. Does that sound fair to you?

Is there a disparity of treatment here based on the skin color of an author, and not the content of his books? Please read on and reason for yourself.

What I saw the discovery in my daughter's case against Penguin prove, was that if you are a black aspiring author, or a black published author, your value and worth are regarded differently than a white author regardless of the content of your work - based solely on your race.

When commercial fiction authors like James Patterson, Sue Monk Kidd, Kathryn Stockett, Suzanne Brockmann, or any other white author, writes black characters, they are not relegated to the African-American niche. But if you are black, your work is not considered by the mainstream publishers to be suitable for the greater, white marketplace, no matter *what* you have written - even when it does not even have black characters! The only exceptions are those who have written literary fiction, such as Stephen L. Carter, Edward P. Jones, Toni Morrison, et al.

That is the outrage. There are no excuses, no stuttering rationalizations, no worrying about who does, or who does not make the best seller's list that can adequately excuse this ugly reality. It is institutional racism and if it's not decried and condemned until it completely stops, we of all races, including blacks, are guilty of condoning the practice.

As I alluded to before, we must step beyond the typical road these conversations tend to go down. As it is, racism is still a very hard topic to discuss productively today, because whenever there is a charge of racism by any non-white person, it's quickly translated by a certain segment of people as the "Race Card" being played, or as whining by "minorities." It is something that's pervasively denied.

Many white Americans truly feel they are not racist. Some often respond with things like, "I'm not a member of the KKK. I don't wear hoods and white sheets. I have never lynched anyone. I'd never use the word 'nigger,' no, never. So I can't be racist. Only bad people are racists, and I'm a good person. Good people are not racists no matter what they may condone or practice. You (the victim) are the bad person for bringing up 'racism' in the first place. Stop whining and just work hard to achieve your goals like everyone else does."

But if black author's are basically being treated like "niggers," as the Millenia Black v. Penguin case proves that they sometimes are, they should not have to grin and bear it to make white Americans (or even other black Americans) comfortable. They have a right to take a stand and demand the same freedom white authors enjoy for themselves, do they not? The fact is: Black authors are being treated like "niggers." My daughter was treated differently, as less-than, solely because she is black. Solely. Why is that? We have to name it. Name it. Otherwise, it's too easily denied.

Herein, I am going to lay out the events of what happened as I witnessed them and understood them to be, and let you, the reader, decide for yourself if the U.S. book industry is providing an *equal opportunity* to all authors. I am writing from memory, to the best of my recollection, and giving my feelings and opinions about what happened in some detail.

From what I saw, because of the overwhelming evidence of discrimination on their part, Penguin Group realized that the odds of them being able to defend the case in court and win it were not in their favor. So they settled the case with my daughter, and gagged her. She discouraged me from writing this book because of the gag and wants no part of it. She can no longer talk about what Penguin Group U.S.A. did to her...but I can. I'm going to talk about everything.

Chapter 1

THE GREAT PRETENDER

My daughter first self-published THE GREAT PRETENDER (TGP) in 2002 with a race-neutral cover. There were no racial depictions on the cover at all. She did not even put her photo on the book. While it was still self-published, she got dozens of e-mails from foreign publishers and movie people in Hollywood, wanting to know if the rights were available. (All of this was solid, documented evidence in her case.) It wasn't picked up for a movie, but it did get picked up by some of the foreign publishers: Polish, Turkish, and Czech. Remember: this is when the book was *self-published*. To my understanding, this was a remarkable achievement for a self-published novel by an unknown author.

Once Penguin Group U.S.A. acquired it back in 2004 and essentially black-washed it, there were no further foreign language sales, and no more movie inquiries. None. Now, how do you think this would have looked to a jury in court? And would Penguin want to risk finding out?

To prove that the content of TGP is universal and not of a specific culture or race, these foreign publishers used white models on their editions of the very same book that the U.S. publisher used black models on - and based on e-mail evidence and the deposition of their own employee, Penguin's motive was clearly to narrow the appeal and target black readers only, who make up approximately 14-15% of the reading marketplace. Common sense tells you that if you classify the book as being specifically for black people, you are basically alienating the other 85% of the marketplace.

(Now, this is not to say that my daughter, Nadine, necessarily preferred the white models, but she is interested in whatever will afford her stories access to the *largest possible audience,* and give them the best chance at the greatest success, and in this day and age, white skin is much more synonymous with universal than brown skin. This is demonstrated by the industry practice I mentioned before of "white-washing" the book covers of white authors who write about people of color.

How many not-white writers do you see alongside writers like Danielle Steel or Nora Roberts in terms of success?)

When Nadine's editor at Penguin, Kara Cesare, first sent the cover art for TGP to Nadine and her agent at the time, Sara Camilli, Nadine was shocked to see that they had put black faces on the cover. She wrote back to her editor and objected and pointed out the fact that the book *had no black characters,* and that black models gave a false impression and would suggest to the marketplace that the target audience for the book was black. Nadine wants a rainbow of an audience. She wants *everyone* reading this book, not only black people. Whether they are black, white, brown, yellow, purple, or green, she wants the book marketable to them! And why shouldn't she?

Despite these arguments, e-mails revealed that Kara Cesare's boss at the time, Kara Welsh, said she didn't want to "miss out" on the audience they really wanted to target with THE GREAT PRETENDER and that she felt black readers would be "alienated" if the cover didn't have black models.

At the time, my daughter wanted to know: why were they targeting a *black* audience with this book in the first place? It is a family relationship book about infidelity and betrayal. Are these topics exclusive to black people? Would Kara Welsh have been equally as worried about "alienating" the *black* audience if THE GREAT PRETENDER had been written by a white writer? I think this is a fair question, and one that would have been addressed to a jury, too.

It was at the time of this incident that Nadine discovered that editor Kara Cesare had previously asked agent Sara Camilli if Nadine was black or white. (I believe this had been asked shortly after the closing of the book deal, but I could be off on the timing.) To my understanding, Sara Camilli represented other authors at Penguin and they all happen to be black. Since THE GREAT PRETENDER did not have black characters, Kara Cesare found it necessary to ask Sara whether or not Nadine was black. I believe this is why the question was asked, but should there ever be a reason for an editor to need to question whether or not an author is white? Should the editor and publisher not be focused upon the content of the material they have acquired?

My daughter was crushed at the time Kara Welsh made her final decision to ignore the objection and go ahead with the black models anyway.

(Nadine later found out during the discovery process that her agent played a greater role in why Penguin may not have backed down on this first act of discrimination; but more light on the agent's role later with some cautionary advice for all writers in the triangle relationship with their agent and editor.)

Penguin went on to sell rights for THE GREAT PRETENDER to Black Expressions Book Club, a club that targets black readers and has a predominantly black membership, and to the black imprint of Recorded Books, Griot, for the audio version.

Yet in their defendants' response to the allegations made in my daughter's complaint (documents you can find on public record filed in New York federal court), Penguin denied that they labeled and classified her work as *African-American* or *black*. Yet to my understanding, there was more than one e-mail uncovered during the discovery phase of the case in which Kara Cesare and her bosses, Claire Zion and Kara Welsh, were discussing this very classification - they were discussing how they wanted to target black audiences with Millenia Black's books. They apparently saw this as logical and reasonable because Millenia Black is *black*, after all. It didn't matter what she wrote, *she herself*, was black.

I believe there was one e-mail where Kara Cesare told agent Sara Camilli that although they knew THE GREAT PRETENDER could appeal to a wider audience, they wanted to make Millenia Black the female *Eric Jerome Dickey*. (Eric Dickey is a successful Penguin author who has a predominantly black niche audience. I wondered why they wouldn't want to make Millenia the female Nicholas Sparks? He writes similar content and is much more successful than Eric Jerome Dickey, but based on their own words, Millenia was the wrong color for them to have such a lofty aspiration for her. Even though she did not write black content, she was only compared to other blacks.)

Nadine pointed out to them that she did not write the same content as Eric Jerome Dickey, and so the only similarity Penguin was going on was *authors' race*. They were ignoring the content of her book! But this did not stop Penguin. They were the ones in control, and they felt justified and comfortable with making such a decision, because Nadine is black. Do you see why I say there is a mindset that needs changing? They apparently don't see a problem with their reasoning at all, or the harm that it inflicts.

How successful or unsuccessful would THE GREAT PRETENDER have become if it hadn't been handled discriminatorily by Penguin? Now we'll never know. What we do know is that Nadine was robbed of the opportunity and treatment Penguin gives white authors to find out. White authors have the luxury of getting their books handled by content, not by race.

Even when white authors write predominately black characters, their books are either white-washed, as I mentioned before, or like Penguin's author Sue Monk Kidd, they are given an opportunity to debut as runaway bestsellers. Why wasn't THE SECRET LIFE OF BEES, which has mostly black characters, targeted at black readers? Why didn't Penguin use black models on the cover of this book so that black readers wouldn't be "alienated"?

I understand that during the depositions, Penguin was trying to explore and make the argument that the pseudonym "Millenia Black" made it obvious to readers that the book was for a black audience. Yet they were silent when confronted with the fact that they have an author using the pseudonym "Shayla Black" but was not restricting her books to the African-American fiction "publishing ghetto." Isn't a disparity in treatment and opportunity clear to see here?

I also want to mention that in an interview in the back of the Penguin edition of THE GREAT PRETENDER, Nadine took that opportunity to express her aspirations as an author. She expressed how she wanted to have a "boundless appeal." Why did her publisher see fit to erect racial boundaries for her and limit her appeal?

I think that's what hurts the most about this race issue in commercial publishing. A black writer has no control whatsoever over his or her race. But because they are black, their writing career is set in a certain direction by the powers-that-be, in this case, Penguin Group. Talent, luck and hard work does not matter. Race does. There is no way that a black commercial fiction writer can be marketed like author Diana Peterfreund and share the same readers, no matter the quality of what they have written. As you can see, it's a separate, and unequal, career path from any of the commercial white authors. And it's entirely out of their control. This is what hurts the most.

Chapter 2

THE GREAT BETRAYAL

My daughter had contracted for two books with Penguin Group U.S.A. THE GREAT BETRAYAL (TGB) was the second one.

She was so heartbroken about what happened to THE GREAT PRETENDER, that she decided to write the second book specifically identifying that the characters were white. I understand that there are several writers of color who do this, including bestselling author Tess Gerritsen, who I was told encouraged Nadine to do it for a chance at the larger marketplace in which she enjoys great success. Tess Gerritsen has been a great champion of Nadine's and is a wonderful lady who blogs about this problem and apparently wants to see it remedied, as I do. (Tess Gerritsen has said on her blog that even she has been berated by many in the "Asian-American" community for aiming at the larger marketplace by writing white characters. But she does it because it is a harsh (unspoken) reality that we live in a pro-white society, and white characters are considered mainstream, while Asian or black characters are not. This is what must change.)

Now, in the beginning of 2006 when Nadine turned THE GREAT BETRAYAL in to her editor Kara Cesare, her agent Sara Camilli called to say that Kara wanted the characters' race changed to either black, or unspecified, the same way she had written them in THE GREAT PRETENDER. And she said they would not publish the book if the characters were specified as white because the black audience to whom they had marketed Millenia Black's first book (against her wishes) would not buy the second if it was specified that it was about white characters.

As I understand it, around this time, Kara Cesare also provided Sara Camilli with the cover art Penguin intended to use on THE GREAT BETRAYAL, and again, it featured black models. Additionally, as they had done with TGP, Penguin again sold TGB to the Black Expressions book club, and to Griot, the African-American imprint of Recorded Books.

Again, Nadine objected and let them know in no uncertain terms that she was being racially discriminated against since they would never be imposing such a thing on a white author.

It was at this point in 2006 that my daughter got an attorney who served Penguin with a letter, asking that they withdraw their demand of the race change, and that they change the cover of TGB to one that was race-neutral, and accurate to its content. As I understand it, Penguin then agreed to withdraw the demand, but proceeded to distribute the *black* cover in advance to book reviewers and booksellers everywhere, stamping THE GREAT BETRAYAL as an African-American fiction book when all the characters are white. So Nadine felt forced to file the lawsuit against Penguin to maintain her dignity, and to get justice and equal treatment.

There was also a backlash from many black readers against Nadine for writing THE GREAT BETRAYAL about white characters. I remember how bad a lot of the comments were that were left on the Black Expressions club website. They felt she was a "race traitor" and should not be trying to reach a white audience. Furthermore, many other members complained that TGB did not belong in the Black Expressions club at all. It was a very sad and sorry situation.

How successful or unsuccessful would THE GREAT BETRAYAL have become if it hadn't been handled discriminatorily by Penguin? Now we will never know. It is my opinion that Penguin's discriminatory actions ruined Millenia Black's writing career. Her chances at reaching a commercial audience with her books was savagely ruined by treatment she never would have received if she were white.

It is important to note: Blacks are published in numbers in commercial fiction now. They were barely being published at all a mere 15-20 years ago. So it goes without saying that things have improved and progressed. However, I think it has been said very well before. So I will quote as follows with a few word replacements to reflect the parallels with today:

There are those who are asking the devotees of civil rights, "When will you be satisfied?" We can never be satisfied as long as [black writers] are the victims of the unspeakable horrors of [publisher] brutality. We can never be satisfied as long as our [books], cannot gain [equal access to the mainstream, commercial bestsellers' lists]. We cannot be satisfied as long as the [black writer's] basic mobility is from a smaller [publishing] ghetto to a larger one. We can never be satisfied as long as our children are stripped of their self-hood and robbed of their dignity by [invisible] signs stating: "For Whites Only."...No, no, we are not satisfied, and we will not be satisfied until "justice rolls down like waters, and righteousness like a mighty stream." - **Excerpts from "I Have a Dream" by Dr. Martin Luther King, Jr. (Speech delivered August 28, 1963)**

Can you see how although much has changed since the institution of slavery, in reality nothing has really changed? Nothing changes until we have true equality among human beings, and no one is making distinctions that pit one skin color above another.

Yes, much progress has been made, but it is not enough when parents must watch their children be stripped of their dignity as my daughter was by Penguin. Before, there was no cause for black authors to complain about separate and unequal writing career opportunities, because they rarely *had* any commercial writing opportunities at all. Now they have the African-American niche to thank for even being published in greater numbers at all. They can thank the niche for the "black" fiction bestsellers' lists, and for the fact that they can read a variety of fiction that feature black main characters.

The African-American niche is considered to be a good thing by many black readers and writers. But those who think it's so good that it usurps a person's right to equal treatment are fools. I have heard many people voice opinions that speak in favor of "Jim Crow" styled publishing. They attacked my daughter for having the audacity to write THE GREAT BETRAYAL, a book with all white characters. Is this not an attempt to strip her of creative freedom? Is this a good thing to do? Why do you think these people want to limit her, an American writing about Americans? These misguided thinkers are in favor of separate, but equal, because they draw their identity from their color, but they need to see that such a way of life is completely impractical. It can never happen. They tried it after slavery and right up through to the 1960's and what happened? One side always got the better end of the stick. It won't work. All people must be united and fight for equal treatment for each other, just as they would for themselves.

Many black authors did not support Nadine's lawsuit against Penguin, because they feared that the case might lead to the industry doing away with the African-American fiction niche, which would take away the one little narrow opening they had to get scraps from the table. They were terrified that publishers would just stop publishing blacks, period. It would be considered too much of a hassle...and, of course, it never occurs to the powerful publishers to just start treating everyone equal and throw the whole race matter out of their minds. So they fear that books with black characters would become a rarity unless white authors wrote them.

So is it any wonder why the bulk of black writers keep their mouths shut and heads down about racism in publishing? I have an interesting behavioral anecdote to share later in the book that speaks to this, but in my opinion there's nothing necessarily wrong with having a black fiction niche. The niche in and of itself actually has nothing to do with racism or segregation. There are shared cultural experiences that make it a valid genre. The problem is how the books are categorized as *black*. If the content of a book in the black fiction niche is ethnic and cultural in tone, then naturally it speaks as its genre. But when the tone of the book is indistinguishable from any other romance, mystery, horror, family saga - or as in my daughter's case, it doesn't even contain a single black character - it obviously doesn't belong in this *black* niche. THE GREAT BETRAYAL (and TGP) have no business being categorized as *black* or *African-American*.

You would think this would be a given, common sense, but it is not how the publishing industry presently operates. **A book should be categorized by its content, not by the race of the author.** It is so wrong to categorize books by the author's race, yet this is exactly - exactly - what Penguin did to Nadine. The painful and sad part is that they did not do this by accident. The written e-mail evidence was clear, they knew they were acting discriminatorily, but they felt *justified and entitled* to do it anyway. How could they even think of opening their mouths to tell her they would not publish THE GREAT BETRAYAL with white characters? This is the outrage.

Author Suzanne Brockmann has written several books with black characters. Why aren't they in the *black* niche along with the other black character romances? Why does Suzanne Brockmann receive special, or more beneficial, treatment? Author Sue Monk Kidd did the same with THE SECRET

LIFE OF BEES, yet she was also not positioned for the *black* fiction niche.

But quite conversely, the black author who wrote THE GREAT BETRAYAL with no black characters was automatically relegated to the *black* niche, complete with a black cover. Why should Nadine's (or any other author's) skin color be relevant to the audience her book gains access to?

Chapter 3

THE AGENT

Based on this experience, I want to offer a word of advice to any writer who is reading this book. Whether you are represented by an agent at the moment or not, keep this in mind: unless you are anywhere near as successful a writer as, let's say, Danielle Steel and her equals in the book business, it's very unlikely that your agent is actually representing *you* to your publisher. In reality, the agent is often representing the *publisher* to *you*. You are expendable, whereas the giant publishing company is not.

The way the book industry was established and orchestrated to work, is that agents need the publishers far more than they need you! If they upset an editor(s) at one publishing house, that agent can probably kiss off any chance of selling another book to that publisher ever again. So while you believe your agent is advocating for your views, opinions, and directives, something quite different can be happening during his or her actual communications with the publisher.

How does a struggling writer overcome this vulnerability and disadvantage? My advice is to make sure you communicate *directly* with your editor at the publishing company. Make sure you are not solely relying on your agent. Of course, you must use good discretion, you don't want your agent to think you don't trust him or her, but when it comes to anything of importance to you during the process, make sure you communicate your desires and opinions to the publisher *directly*.

I hope you don't have to end up in court with your publisher, but in the event that you do, you don't want them to make an argument that they didn't know exactly what you wanted...and your agent will be more likely to back them up than to back you up! For an agent, it's crucial to the health of their business, and to the other authors they may already have with that publisher.

My daughter's agent, Sara Camilli, tried to do this to stay in Penguin's good graces. What saved Nadine in her case, were the e-mails she had sent *directly* to her editor Kara Cesare expressing her objections to their handling of her books. If she had relied on Sara's communication with them alone, I think her case would've been dismissed, because I understand that e-mails were uncovered that showed that agent Sara Camilli was telling Kara Cesare how Nadine would be a "team player" and go along with anything Penguin decided. This was unbeknownst to my daughter. It was a good thing she had been e-mailing her feelings to Kara Cesare directly. So Cesare could not simply claim ignorance and go by what the agent said alone.

See what happens? If the agent can make you look like a "team player" and not cause the publisher too much of a headache, the agent stays in their good graces while returning to you, the author, saying things like, "Sorry the publisher made their final decision, you have to live with it." So the agent comes out smelling like a rose, right?

When she was being deposed in this case, as I understand it, Sara Camilli had a hell of a time explaining why there was a contradiction between what Nadine had told her in e-mails and what she was representing to Penguin. I believe that one of the things she said by way of excuse, was that she spoke with Nadine *over the phone* and got the impression she would be *willing* to go along with Penguin's decision - from conversations they had over the phone. Yet the history of the written documents did not support this claim at all. Camilli knew she was in trouble, and so I think she was doing everything she could during the case to cooperate with the process and make nice to Nadine, and apologize. I don't think Camilli wanted to be the next one sued, for misrepresentation.

Now, I am really not here to disparage agent Sara Camilli, just to share my knowledge and feelings about some of her actions as they were discovered to be in the course of this dispute, and how it can be useful to other writers. As I see it, she was clearly looking to protect *her business* and had more reason to side with Penguin than with my daughter, to whom she had a fiduciary responsibility as a literary agent, not to mention as a human being. I think she failed in her responsibility and knows she could have been sued for it based on the e-mails. I know that Nadine had written proof, e-mail communication history, that proved she was in no way willing to go along with Penguin's ghettoizing of her work, yet based on the evidence, Sara Camilli got caught telling them she would, lying to keep The Sara Camilli Agency in Penguin Group's good favor.

When I consider what could have happened if my daughter had not had those e-mails, I cringe. So again: I cannot stress enough that writers must protect themselves and remember to communicate directly with their publisher about things that are important to them. Do not rely on the agent's communications alone. A writer is never as important to an agent's business as a publisher is. It seems that's just the way the clever founders of the publishing industry positioned things to be. At every turn, it is set up in favor of the publishing giants, and agents are at their mercy...not yours.

To my knowledge, the majority of Sara Camilli's authors were black and all of the writers she represented with Penguin were black and this is what prompted Penguin to overlook the content of her books and ask about my daughter's race. It seemed to me that Camilli's experience in the publishing industry was limited to the success she enjoyed representing authors like Zane and Eric Jerome Dickey. She seemed to expect Nadine to aim to reach for their level of success and not to think of aiming higher. That is the impression I had of her, based on the kind of counsel and advice she was giving my daughter.

There was also an e-mail exchange I saw between Camilli and Kara Cesare where Camilli was singing the praises of THE GREAT PRETENDER and its foreign appeal. She told Cesare that it was amazing that Nadine was getting so many foreign rights queries while this didn't happen for her other authors and she wondered why.

I think I can guess why...could it be that THE GREAT PRETENDER was written in a more universal way than her other authors wrote in? Could it be that the foreign marketplace was an open field for Millenia Black's book, a marketplace to which agent Sara Camilli helped Penguin limit her appeal?

Well, I think that is most evidently what happened. Ever since Penguin's black-washed edition came out, my daughter has received no more foreign interest queries.

Chapter 4

THE EDITOR

I must say that, based on what I heard, my daughter's editor, Kara Cesare, tried to get Nadine what she wanted in the beginning, but she was overruled by her bosses at Penguin, Claire Zion and Kara Welsh. They had the final word and then poor Kara had to enforce it. I think she felt terrible about the whole episode and was just doing the job Penguin gave her to do.

Is she a racist? I don't know, but I do know she played a racist role against my daughter when she told her to change the characters in THE GREAT BETRAYAL from white to black, or to not specify the race so they could repeat the treatment they gave to THE GREAT PRETENDER. I call this racist because I believe that when she was deposed, Kara Cesare admitted that she has never told one of her white authors to do this or risk not having their book published!

I understand that during her deposition, Kara Cesare also had a very difficult time explaining why a book that contained no African-American characters would be packaged and marketed by Penguin as if it did. When asked why THE GREAT PRETENDER was on the market the way Penguin had released it, I believe she said that she pictured the characters as being African-American because agent Sara Camilli told her that they were. But I know that Camilli, during her own deposition, had no choice but to deny she told Kara any such thing. The reason that Sara had to admit this was because there was some written e-mail evidence of Sara saying it before. (I believe that Camilli testified that she never thought of race when she read THE GREAT PRETENDER because none had been specified, and she thought the characters could have been anyone.)

To my understanding, editor Kara Cesare also testified that she never *demanded* that Nadine change the race of the characters in THE GREAT BETRAYAL, that she only "suggested" it because she thought that's what Nadine *wanted*. (So if that were true, why was she now giving a deposition in a race discrimination lawsuit?)

And when my daughter's attorney confronted Cesare with the e-mail in which she tells Nadine of her demand to make the race change, she says she made a mistake and didn't mean to say that it was a *demand,* or imply that they wouldn't go ahead with publishing the book as it was written. She testified that it was really meant as a harmless suggestion and not meant as any form of racial discrimination. But she denied having ever told one of her white authors to do the same.

Now how do you think all this might have gone over in court? Do you think a jury would've believed Kara Cesare? I don't think Penguin was too eager to find that out.

Chapter 5

THE PUBLICIST

My daughter's publicist at Penguin was named Paola something. Sorry, I don't remember her last name. She was to be a key witness in Nadine's case. She was willing to testify to the internal business practices she witnessed as an employee of Penguin that showed how treating authors according to race was actually an extremely *big part* of Penguin Group U.S.A.'s business model.

As I understand it, Paola had said she was known internally as the publicist who mostly handled the "minority authors." In other words, if an author got her as a publicist, they were usually not white.

She also told my daughter's attorney, as I understand it, that whether an author is black or white determines everything from who handles it throughout the production process, to the venues the sales team targets for selling the books. It affected how much of an advance the author would get and how much their print run would be. For instance, a debut novelist who was white might easily get a $50,000 advance at Penguin, while a debut novelist who happen to be black or Hispanic might be lucky if they got $10,000. The size of the target audience makes all the difference to how much money they project the book will make back. These divides are pretty much standard throughout the whole of the publishing industry.

Now how can a non-white author compete with that if their work is being handled according to race and not content?

I believe Paola had left Penguin to go work for another publisher by the time the lawsuit was filed, but this lady was very willing to testify to what she experienced inside Penguin Group, because she didn't think it was equitable at all. I think she told Nadine that Penguin's lawyers contacted her and it seemed like they were trying to coerce her into covering up certain details of the internal process, and trying to get her to speak in Penguin's favor.

But Paola never got to be deposed. I think Nadine's lawyer had scheduled the deposition, but Penguin chose to settle the case with my daughter before it happened.

Chapter 6

THE LAWYERS

According to Wikipedia (http://en.wikipedia.org/wiki/White_supremacy), "**White supremacy** is the belief that white people are superior to people of other racial backgrounds."

I do not believe that most of our country is filled with people who believe this consciously. I do believe, however, that you are hard-pressed to find anyone in America who does not believe this *subconsciously,* because of the pro-white atmosphere in which all Americans are raised up. But due to the ugly nature of the mindset, most will verbally deny they believe in it, while promoting it through their actions.

When my daughter first sought legal counsel for this matter, some lawyers laughed her off the phone. They told her that they saw no reason for a publisher to hinder its own chance to make money by limiting her books to black audiences. Yet this is *exactly* what Penguin did.

When Nadine initially filed the complaint, she bravely did so pro se, acting as her own attorney. She didn't have the thousands of dollars most lawyers wanted in order to take the case, and she couldn't find any willing to take it on contingency. They told her that it was an unprecedented application of the civil rights law, and that it was too risky because a corporation like Penguin Group had the pockets to drag the case on for years.

I recall that a couple of attorneys were willing to take it if they could find a solid expert witness, someone qualified to speak to the racial divide of book publishing, with hard facts and data to back up the charge that Penguin did not take such actions with white authors. The revelation to me here was that the publishing corporations have such great power that it intimidates many who could help remedy this situation. It's not only The Oprah Show producers who are afraid to touch this, but even retired professionals who no longer work in the industry.

As I understand it, it was not until nearly two years into the case that Nadine's lawyer was able to find an expert witness who was willing to testify in court. And her lawyer took the case out of the goodness of his heart. It is not easy to find attorneys who will work at a reduced rate to help your cause, but Nadine was finally able to find one to sign on and take over from her. She was representing herself well enough, but knew she still needed to find a good attorney to go up against the sharks Penguin had hired to represent them.

I won't beleaguer the brutal legal process, as it is common knowledge how vicious unscrupulous, big-firm lawyers can be, and Penguin's vipers were no exception. It was obvious to me that they had no way out except to play dirty, and try to harass and intimidate my daughter with irrelevant subpoenas for information from her job, her Alma Mater, her family members, you name it, they sent subpoenas. They insisted on doing a search of her personal computer to try and dig into her private life. Where was the relevance in all of this? Nothing could change the glaring fact that my daughter's books contained not one single black character, yet they had been style, published, and marketed as if they did. Were they doing that to the white authors who had not written about black characters? They don't even do it to the white authors who do!

So what do you think was the point of all the harassment? I think they wanted to exhaust my daughter's attorney, who they knew she wasn't able to pay much for his time. I think they were hoping to wear them down so Nadine would give up. But Penguin didn't know who they were dealing with. They were dealing with someone who had the truth on her side and was not easily intimidated, and would not just drop the case and run away.

It seemed to me that they really panicked after editor Kara Cesare's deposition, as I discussed back in Chapter 4. The evidence of racial treatment with Millenia Black's books was overwhelmingly damning.

Some things that I found interesting about the discovery phase was how Penguin's attorneys tried to question my daughter about *my* past during her deposition, when I was not even a party to the case! And I understand that they also questioned her about why she chose the name "Reginald" for the lead character in THE GREAT PRETENDER. Apparently implying that it was a *black* person's name, and to my understanding, Nadine proceeded to give them a list of white men named "Reginald," including Sir Elton John, himself! Now, don't you think that is a shame? Is there a white author who would be forced to endure such a demeaning question about their story?

Why didn't Penguin just take responsibility for their actions and acknowledge that they had treated the author racially? I believe this speaks to a deeper problem. The problem being that many white people have been historically conditioned to feel a natural sense of superiority over non-white people, and as such, they feel they have every right to exert such discriminatory power in business as long as they see fit. And they don't see any reason to make any apologies for it.

I think the decent thing would have been for Penguin to offer to republish her books properly - the same way they publish the books written by white authors. They do not do so with an aim at limiting them to the "African American" marketplace.

But instead, they hire lawyers to try and humiliate her with questions like why a character is named "Reginald," or why she chose "Millenia Black" for her pseudonym. Is this the way the publishers in the great country of America should treat their writers? I think it's a shame!

Chapter 7

THE RAMIFICATIONS

The reason this situation is important and warrants the writing of this book, is because it has implications that go beyond just Millenia Black and Penguin.

My daughter felt very strongly that it was important to take a stand against Penguin's treatment of her work, and not to take the advice that her agent and others were giving her.

Her agent, Sara, encouraged her to let Penguin go ahead and pigeonhole Millenia Black as an author of African-American fiction, and try to circumvent the system by writing another book and using another pseudonym to publish it, and Sara promised that she would not reveal that the author was black to the editors she submitted this new book to. I understand that Sara told my daughter to wait until she was forty-years-old to expect any great success in the book business. Nadine told me that she refused that advice because she should not have to do that. She had already written two universal and mainstream books. Are white authors being told to take another pseudonym and write more so they could hide their race from editors and avoid being treated disparately?

The ramifications of the racial divide purported by the publishing giants is a diminishing of human beings and their dignity. Why subject some to limiting treatment while others enjoy unlimited freedom? And should those who are thus subjected keep quiet about it? Should they just accept it? Many do accept it. They are afraid to lose the little that they have.

I learned so many things as I watched my daughter go through this terrible experience. Did you know that the number of copies a publisher prints (called a print-run) of a book can help or hurt its chances for success? This is one of the things I learned from the discovery process of the case and one of the thing's Nadine's publicist, Paola, was set to testify about.

It seems that a publisher can show the booksellers and media how much they are backing one of their new releases by the number of copies they say they are going to print. The debut of a white author's book may get an initial print run of anywhere from 20,000 to 100,000 copies. A non-white author's debut is lucky if it gets 7,000 copies.

Does this provide an equal opportunity for success?

Another place to find evidence of the racial divide in publishing is in the advance that is paid to authors. I learned that a white debut author may get anywhere from a $20,000.00 - $150,000.00 advance. Whereas a black debut author is lucky to get a $10,000.00 advance.

I remember there were also e-mails that were uncovered during the discovery phase that Kara Cesare and her boss Claire Zion sent to each other and to agent Sara Camilli, in which the advances they pay to Sara's authors were being discussed, along with the fact that her authors were all black. It seems her authors typically get $10,000.00 advances, and that's it. Sara asked them for $20,000.00 to show that they really believed in Millenia Black above the rest of her authors.

Does this imbalance in the amount of advances paid reflect equal treatment? Equal opportunity?

How can an author who is not white ever expect to achieve the same level of success that an author who is white is able to achieve when they are being treated in such uneven ways?

Why aren't more people outraged about this present-day "Jim Crow" type of system?

A CALL TO ACTION

I acknowledge that many of the writers who are negatively affected by this divide are too afraid to fight back as my daughter did. Not everyone has the strength or the great fortitude to do it. But it is time to call on everyone, whether you are black, white, Asian, Native American, Hispanic, everyone - we must acknowledge and decry these practices. It's time to stop being passive supporters of a white supremacist society. We should all be in favor of the right to equal opportunity. I firmly believe that it is what is written in a book that should determine its genre, and the audience that should be targeted. As my daughter's situation proves, this is not what the publishers are doing.

The conscious, or unconscious, exalting of white writers above non-white writers is an assault on the whole American society. I know it brings up guilt and other negative emotions in many white people to hear non-white people say they are being racially discriminated against.

The backlash for speaking out can be brutal. I witnessed it firsthand when it happened to my child.

When Nadine first became vocal about what Penguin was doing to her, there were some in the blog world who immediately met her situation with angry skepticism, demanding proof that she had even filed a lawsuit against Penguin and casting doubt that any of her claims were true...

Tell me, how can a book that has no black characters get plastered with a black cover and not be proof of racial discrimination? But this fact was ignored by these "skeptics" and my daughter was impugned and humiliated by these people. And were they even truly skeptical? I don't think so at all. I honestly believe it is either a subconscious sense of superiority, or a subconscious sense of guilt (or a combination of both), that drives many whites to anger at the mere mention of racism from any black person. It then becomes their duty to make the victim out to be a liar who is looking to make progress without working hard to achieve it the way white people do. They are determined to stomp the victim of racism into the ground to deny and hide the problem, rather than acknowledge the fact that the mere look of their skin gives them an unearned advantage, and then work together to level the playing field for their fellow Americans.

I can only imagine how hard it is for those who are privileged to willingly take action to lose such privilege, or to even acknowledge the fact that they have it.

The "skeptics" who I felt displayed the most anger and viciousness toward Nadine when she talked about what was happening to her (almost as if she had done something to harm them personally) were popular industry bloggers Ed Champion (edrants.com), and Lynne Scanlon (thepublishingcontrarian.com).

Mr. Ed Champion started out positively on his blog by saying that if what Millenia Black said was true, Penguin's actions were wrong on many levels. He said he was investigating the situation by making calls and sending e-mails to the folks at Penguin (which he did, as his e-mails became a part of the discovery in the case), and he even interviewed my daughter for a podcast he said he was doing on the subject. But soon thereafter, Champion turned negative and began to shift the focus to Nadine's use of a pseudonym to write under, and then he posted on his blog that he was no longer interested in Millenia Black's case because her "veracity" was in question. And the reason? Well, he said that the other blogger, Lynne Scanlon's, speculations came closest to the reason.

This is what his blog post says at http://edrants.com/?p=4661:

"Housekeeping #1: For those who have emailed me on the Millenia Black story this past week, after several conversations calling into question the veracity of what has been claimed, I have decided to stop pursuing it. I have neither the time nor the inclination to proceed further — unless, of course, a reputable publication pays me to write an investigative article. But if you remain curious as to the why, Lynne Scanlon comes the closest in her speculations."

Now, Ms. Lynne Scanlon's position was that Millenia Black's complaint was without merit because it's all about marketing, not race. She said that forcing Millenia Black to have her books styled and marketed only for black people - even when the books have no black characters - is just good business on Penguin's part. Her blog post can be found here: http://www.thepublishingcontrarian.com/2006/10/17/are-black-authors-getting-nigger-treatment-is-niche-a-dirty-word-is-millenia-black-really-suing-penguin-group-over-white-v-black-characters/

Her reasoning seems to be that an author should market himself by whatever he has to offer that's unique, including his ethnicity. Is this just a convenient way to excuse racial discrimination by those in positions of power? In this case, Penguin? It sounds like a shallow excuse to me. It sounds like she is basically giving them (white people) the right to put black faces on the cover of a book with no black content simply because the author of the book is a black person. Does the mentality of the U.S. Supreme Court's ruling in Dred Scott v. Sandford not shine through right here? Scanlon is basically casting Penguin in the role of the 1857 Supreme Court and Millenia Black as Dred Scott. Can you see how subconscious racism must be at play here in the 2000's? Would Scanlon admit it outright that she gives the publisher the discretion to treat their authors unequally based on their race, or would she cloak this belief in assertions about "good marketing" and profit by any means necessary?

Only black authors are limited and segregated into a racial niche. They cannot use their ethnicity as a writer to appeal to a market without being shoved into a box, or a publishing ghetto, where only that particular group of people can see their work. The Irish example that Lynne Scanlon used in her blog post is completely irrelevant. Irish (or other ethnicity) authors are not marketed *solely* to Irish readers, and shelved in an *Irish* section of the bookstore, no matter how much they may use their ethnicity in the marketing.

Now does this reaction make Ed Champion and Lynne Scanlon racists? Or are they just consistently skeptical people by nature? To my knowledge, neither has reacted this way to the white authors like Justine Larbalestier and Jaclyn Dolamore, when their work was white-washed by their publisher. Now while Champion and Scanlon (and the mindset they represent) may not be consciously racist, much can be gleaned from their speech, what they have to say. Subconscious guilt, or a subconscious sense of superiority, tends to spark anger and resentment in a lot of white people.

The words of one of the former Presidents of the United States, Woodrow Wilson, go as follows:

"The white men were roused by a mere instinct of self-preservation...until at last there had sprung into existence a great Ku Klux Klan, a veritable empire of the South, to protect the Southern country."
- History of the American People

"A veritable empire..." This is the truth no one wants to touch in the present-day discussions about racism in America. The fact that this was the way our own government thought and spoke openly and freely about people of color as recent as the early 1900's, affirms a painful truth about today's atmosphere. This was a President of the United States speaking, and it was not that long ago. Can you see how the legacy of this kind of thinking is still among us and being perpetuated today? Yes, it is in a watered down form, but nonetheless, many white people have inherited, and live according to, some form of this belief system.

This type of mindset won't be interested to investigate or research enough to know that the issue with the racial divide in publishing isn't the existence of the African-American niche for marketing. If the content is ethnic in nature, sure, why not the niche? Then it is logical and appropriate. There isn't anything wrong with appealing to people because of shared cultural experience. What *is* wrong is when the writer is forced into a box and the content of their book is automatically disregarded. Books such as ANGELA'S ASHES by Frank McCourt sit with the bulk of other books in the mainstream; it is not in its own section. Neither is the THE JOY LUCK CLUB by Amy Tan. It's only the bulk of black writers who are being set apart, with very shallow justifications for this marginalization.

As I mentioned before, only a chosen few black literary authors like Toni Morrison and Maya Angelou are deemed *universal* and get accepted to sit among the other books. Yet, the (subconscious) racist mindset tends to cloud the issue with angry, shallow arguments, because they don't care to acknowledge their privilege, particularly as such privilege comes so natural and reasonable to their way of life.

Shouldn't everyone want books to be categorized by content? If fiction is primarily ethnicity-based, such as street literature, or so-called "street-lit," then, yes, it limits itself as a primarily African-American interest. But why should a mystery or family saga written by a black author go in that category? Why isn't the author just a mystery author if he wrote a mystery? Or an author of women's fiction if that's what she writes? Sure, publishers want to use any uniqueness about a writer to market their books: cultural background, shared experience, etc. Other authors do this, too. But the question is:

Why can't an author who happens to be black be a mystery writer just like all the other mystery writers? From the likes of Tony Hillerman to James Patterson, they are not treated like *black* authors by their publishers, though the ethnicity of their characters are often not white. Why?

I want to point out that, of course, this isn't an issue that is exclusive the Ed Champions and Lynne Scanlons of the world, but I underscore their commentary about my daughter's case, as they represent the mindset I'm speaking of, the people who have unearned personal privilege as a result of the skin color they were born with. I don't know who Ed Champion and Lynne Scanlon are, but I would guess that they are white and thus have absolutely no worries about the pain a black author suffers as a result of the racism in publishing. What do you think? Much like how scores of Germans stood by in Nazi Germany, right? It's not an issue to many white Americans how their fellow non-white Americans are being treated. Mr. Champion's angry feelings about my daughter were apparently so strong that I read a post on his blog where he went so far as to mock the pain of her victimization by Penguin. He actually sat down and took the time to spit on her, basically. You can read that post at this address: http://www.edrants.com/a-hack-of-a-different-stripe/

I can tell you that it bothered me as a father much more than it bothered Nadine. It seemed very mean-spirited of Mr. Ed, to me, for him to ignore what Penguin did to my daughter's books, in favor of changing the whole subject of the problem to inflate his clear sense of superiority.

(**Note:** Just in case any of the Web posts that I am citing should be removed from the blogs, I want to refer you to the Wayback Machine at (http://www.archive.org.) Nothing posted on the internet is ever lost. All Web addresses are archived there. My daughter had posted her feelings on her blog, discussing her struggles, and I can no longer find them on her blog, but I can access them via the Wayback Machine:

http://milleniablack.blogspot.com/2006/04/great-betrayal-jim-crow-publishing.html
http://milleniablack.blogspot.com/2006/10/great-lawsuit.html)

Many minority authors (not all) got excited about my daughter taking a stand because they also want equal access for success. Most don't have the huge amounts of money to spend, or the willingness to destroy their dreams and writing careers to directly take on a publisher through the court system. And neither did my daughter. Rosa Parks had an army and movement behind her. And we know that sometimes it takes a Rosa Parks. But there were others, like the author, Zane, who joined in on the attacks against Nadine. Our country's racial atmosphere is such that blacks often police each other against speaking out about racism to those in power. This "policing" manifests in various forms, but in Zane's case I suspect she came out and attacked my daughter because Nadine's position made her feel uncomfortable about her own self. This would be a largely subconscious truth for Zane, and others who are similarly conditioned, I think. Would Zane ever consciously say she didn't believe a black author should have the same treatment as a white? Probably not. But that's basically what I understood her to say in the comments she posted on a message board about the subject. However, Zane cloaked it in angry arguments in favor of a publisher's right to do whatever it wanted with a book it acquired - up to and including racially discriminate against its author.

Here is the anecdote I promised earlier. The story of the Five Monkeys:

There was an interesting experiment that started with five monkeys in a cage. A banana hung inside the cage with a set of steps placed underneath it. After a while, a monkey went to the steps and started to climb towards the banana, but when he touched the steps, he set off a spray that soaked all the other monkeys with cold water. Another monkey tried to reach the banana with the same result. It didn't take long for the monkeys to learn that the best way to stay dry was to prevent any monkey from attempting to reach the banana.

The next stage of the experiment was to remove the spray from the cage and to replace one of the monkeys with a new one. Of course, the new monkey saw the banana and went over to climb the steps. To his horror, the other monkeys attacked him. After another attempt, he learnt that if he touched the steps, he would be assaulted.

Next, another of the original five was replaced with a new monkey. The newcomer went to the steps and was attacked. The previous newcomer joined in the attack with enthusiasm!

Then, a third monkey was replaced with a new one and then a fourth. Every time a newcomer approached the steps, he was attacked. Most of the monkeys beating him had no idea why they were not allowed to climb the steps or why they were joining in the beating of the newest monkey.

*After replacing the fifth monkey, none of the monkeys had ever been sprayed with water. Still, no monkey ever approached the steps. Why not? Because as far as they knew, it was the way it had always been done in the cage...and that is how habitual mindsets develop. **(Portions excerpted from http://www.learningpages.org)***

When white authors speak out against racism, their comments are supported by most other authors. I have not heard anyone attack the author's who spoke out very frankly on the behalf of (white) erotic romance when the romance genre establishment tried to discriminate against *them*. No, they were supported by their peers no matter how forthright, passionate or assertive they expressed what they needed to say. I've observed that black authors don't seem to do the same, even as they are blatantly discriminated against and treated differently because of their race.

If the majority of white writers were being treated the same way in the publishing industry, I think there would be a strong verbal and national outcry against the practices, until such practices stopped. What if their books were being marketed only to a select few, based on some external characteristic they didn't choose? Instead of universally, according to content, as any author who is not black enjoys under the current system?

What if books by Jewish writers, such as Jennifer Weiner, were being marketed only to other Jews, for instance? What if mysteries or thrillers by women, such as Linda Fairstein and Kathy Reichs, were being marketed only to other blonde women? I doubt they would do what Zane did to Millenia Black. They would not likely be criticizing each other for speaking out and trying to improve the imbalance. If their own opportunities were being racially limited, they would not give trivial justifications about marketing possibilities, as they so readily assert about the African-American fiction niche. They would not be silent for fear of offending, or making others uncomfortable. I think they would be screaming and rioting in the streets, demanding reform and equal treatment.

And they'd be supporting each other while they did it.

But habitual traditions hold many people silent. It seems easier to accept the status quo because fighting it is too hard and can come at a high price. Many people are just afraid because they might have to look in the mirror the objection is holding up, and not like the reflection they see. Where is the solidarity? Not just among races, but among human beings? Why does any American stand around, while others are forced to accept racial discrimination, and not say a word against it for fear of being sprayed with "cold water," or risking a severe backlash from all sides?

It's just like the monkeys in the cage.

Among blacks, the entire slave culture was founded on silence, and fostered mistrust of one another. A select few were elevated to the status of "house Negro" and overseer positions, so the rest would have something to aspire to. The foundation of the slave culture counted on the guarantee of the slaves not rebelling, not speaking out or causing trouble. Such behavior was taboo and could get you beaten - or worse - lynched. The "house Negroes" and black overseer's primary responsibilities were to keep the "field negroes" in order. Any Negro who showed any attitude would never, ever get to be (or remain) a "house Negro" at best, and at worse, would be whipped, sold or lynched.

They kept each other in line so that they could keep the flow of their own crumbs coming from the *white* table. They still are. Can you see the watered down version of this mindset as a fixture in our society today? It does not help matters when one author who chooses to write according to race, attacks another who chooses not to. It is a sad state, but even blacks contribute to the problem by insisting other blacks be stripped of the freedom whites are enjoying by default. And then some whites feel justified by this and use it as an excuse for continuing the abuse.

These are the truths that need to be spoken, and badly. But often no one, black or white, will risk it because it's their method of self-preservation. From what I've observed, it seems the racial imbalance in publishing is fine as long as it's not happening to white authors.

Those with a superior mindset enjoy taking umbrage to sort of stoke their feelings of superiority. Those who talk like Ed Champion and Lynne Scanlon are comparable to the fuming whites you see crowded around a hanging black body in old photos of a lynching. Mr. Champion's and Ms. Scanlon's behavior exhibit the watered down version of the very same mindset that used to justify committing murder. I honestly believe that if my daughter's situation had happened in 1906 instead of in 2006, she would be dead right now.

Today in publishing, it manifests as cyberspace lynchings. Can you see? I am not being hyperbolic about the situation. If you are willing to look honestly, you will see it is the generational truth. Whenever controversy breaks out over a celebrity's racist comments, we see nationally the evidence of the mindset I am talking about. Michael Richards, the guy who played Kramer on "Seinfeld," the singer John Mayer, who recently admitted to being racist in his dating preferences, Don Imus with his derogatory comments about the female basketball players, Boston police officer Justin Barnett, who called Professor Henry Gates, Jr. a "jungle monkey," and the list goes on. These events are not the problem. They are the *symptoms* of the problem.

Any black person who tries to stand against institutional racism, like Millenia Black did, becomes a prime target for this mindset. Since the existence of racism means they have a seemingly natural advantage, defending the status quo makes them feel better, and it's a huge source of their self-esteem. Just take note of the obvious satisfaction in Mr. Ed's posting as he spewed out a hefty dose of resentment and mockery, while others, including Ms. Lynne Scanlon, stopped by to leave him comments applauding his handy-work.

We can call the way publishing is treating black writers, as a whole, sound marketing and good business practice, but remember: Slavery was a good business practice, too.

All this illustrates the fact that we have an active legacy that was passed down from the slavery establishment in this country, and it is one very few are willing to talk about. I am hoping that will now change. The mainstream media must stop ignoring these types of occurrences, because we see the evidence of how non-white authors are being denied the same opportunities to reach the New York Times Best Sellers' List that white authors have. The very visible proof astounds me: One white writer after another can debut on the list with books full of black characters because their publishers do not black-wash their books to target only black readers with them. Books like THE SECRET LIFE OF BEES by Sue Monk Kidd and THE HELP by Kathryn Stockett are excellent examples of this. Both of these novels are published by Penguin Group U.S.A.

Can you see the imbalance very clearly now? Do you see why I had to write this book to share these observations? We must all take part in the solution, and the right to freedom for everyone.

As you have more than likely gleaned by now, my feelings about racism are very strong. Especially as a conscientious dad. I raised my daughter as I myself was raised, to see *people*, not races. The only race that exists is the human race. That's how I was raised up. From the days of slavery and lynching, it was humans abusing and killing other humans so that an unearned advantage could be established and maintained, one that continues to plague us to this very day. This is the result of an intellectual deficiency that one learns early on in life, from both parenting and from the established society. The deficiency supports the marginalization of non-whites. The punishment of people for not being white must stop now, and it's up to all of us to stop it.

I believe the publishing industry is a microcosm of our country at large. The United States of America is a country of great ideals and so much is possible here that is not possible in other countries. For this, I love America and so fight to hold her accountable for living up to her valiant ideals.

The country was founded racially unequal, in practice, while speaking of freedom and equality in theory. The quote I gave earlier from former President Woodrow Wilson's book entitled, "History of the American People" was featured in a very popular movie made in 1915 entitled, "The Birth of a Nation." This film promoted white supremacy and portrayed the men of the Ku Klux Klan positively; in fact, they are portrayed as heroes, hence the film uses United States President Woodrow Wilson's quote to support its view.

I point this out as an illustration of how a governmental mindset that was so pervasive and so deeply engrained, can't possibly have vanished overnight. Especially when it was just the other day in the 1960's that desegregation took place. When does America start to live up to its ideals and begin to practice the freedom it says it provides for all? How can there be freedom for all when a white author can debut on the New York Times Best Sellers' List, but a non-white is not afforded the same access to achieve this success?

The following is a statement that my daughter has always felt still applies today. She has posted it on her blog a few times and I think it's fitting to share it here:

"The Negro was to accept the biracial system and his subordinate status. He was to seek advancement within the confines of his segregated black world. He was to develop the friendship of influential whites and use their assistance.

By cultivating habits of hard work, thrift, and honesty, he was to demonstrate his claim to wider acceptance and better treatment. Above all, he was never to present any organized challenge to the existing order of things or engage in movements which might be regarded by whites as detrimental to their economic and political interest." - **Booker T. Washington**

This continues on because of the mentality of We the People. We make up society, so it is us who allow it to go on, we tolerate and/or endure it. For instance, why do the producers at The Oprah Show refuse to pay attention to this problem? When Oprah is such a powerful influence in the book business and can have a significant impact on the racism being practiced there? Why would they see fit to send my letter to Penguin? To alert them to the fact that I was trying to get Oprah's attention, yet they haven't even sent a canned letter response back to me? I feel they are ignoring the blatant racism against Millenia Black while protecting their publishing industry friends and cronies at Penguin who may very well be giving them kickbacks to get Penguin's books in front of Oprah in the hopes she will pick more of them for her book club. Do you see the problem here?

To my understanding, the majority of the Oprah Show's producers are white. Oprah has worked with them for many, many years and I am sure she would not likely believe them to have a racist bone in their bodies. Even her white producers/employees themselves don't likely believe themselves to be in anyway racist. But let's look at the condition of the society they all live in and see how anyone can escape being racially conditioned in some way or another. Do white Americans have a problem with racism? Do Oprah's white employees have a problem with racism?

What kind of relationship can blacks and whites have when they live in a society that is so clearly pro-white in matters of beauty, literature, arts, film, and in almost anything to do with mainstream pop culture. Oprah Winfrey is obviously a black woman. She is the boss of many of these white employees, so in her organization, things would seem to be the opposite of what is true in American society at large...but for white people, the larger society is still in their favor, whether or not they work for a black person. What I am basically highlighting here, is that most white people may not think they have a racist bone in their body, but how can they escape it when they are born and raised in a pro-white society? A society where their color gives them a (mostly) unspoken advantage over other races?

So you can see why it would be quite easy for a white producer's response to Penguin's racist treatment of my daughter to be, "Oprah won't touch this." I certainly don't believe for one second that Oprah, herself, would say such a thing. My daughter has always felt that Oprah is very insulated and is not privy to everything that comes into her company. She relies on her staff to inform her about the issues and topics coming into her business. I don't for one second believe that Oprah herself would have sent my letter to Penguin, or told someone to do such a thing. I believe that could only be the action of someone who is subconsciously racist, as many white people are. Because they are basically indifferent to the plight of those who suffer under a pro-white atmosphere.

Some may feel this is a controversial statement to make, but truth must be spoken if our nation is to heal once and for all: In the case of Oprah Winfrey, and other wealthy black people, they must realize that the whites who work for them are more than likely respectful of their money and related power, above and beyond respecting them as *black* individuals. It reminds me of what Richard Gere's character said to Julia Robert's character in the movie "Pretty Woman." He said, "Stores are nice to credit cards, not people." Well, you can see the parallel.

The societal makeup dictates that this is so. How much respect, admiration and freedom is afforded a poor black? Even less than what is afforded the poor white. When the poor white can write commercial fiction and debut on the New

York Times Best Sellers' List without any obstruction, the poor black cannot. Have I not proven this point?

And it's not just Oprah's people, it's much of the mainstream media. With all the white-washed and black-washed book cover uproars recently, I don't think any of the mainstream media or investigative journalists have paid any attention to these incidents. And it is not because they have not been alerted. I myself have spent many hours alerting them over the years. Everyone from CNN to Good Morning America to The New York Times. I have been ignored. Only Jeff Trachtenberg at the Wall Street Journal wrote that article about the racial divide in publishing back in 2006; that is four years ago now.

I think they are all afraid of making a monster of the publishers because they have too many friends in this particular industry...and they themselves are not suffering as a result of the racism. And, of course, the larger reason is the fact that most of the people in positions of power are white, and many white people in power have no problem with racism since it benefits them and those who look like them.

It is like a psychological illness being handed down generation to generation, and look at the harm and pain it causes. To make so many groups of people feel like they were born inferior because they don't have white skin, it's like they were born to be treated third-class and they must just accept it.

Even when you are not directly affected by discrimination it *is* affecting you. How? If one person's rights can be stripped, all person's rights can be stripped! Don't you see? That even if you are white, and currently have no problem with racism because you are not the one on the down side of the divide, that your freedom is up for grabs as well? The tables can be turned in one hour of life or another once freedom itself can be withheld anywhere. This is why it is a *human* problem and not just a problem for minority groups to try and solve on their own.

It is the virtue of freedom we are fighting for, not an unearned advantage.

I hear people say all the time that we should be happy things are not the way they used to be. Slavery could still be legal in America and family members being sold away to other white plantation owners. People could still be sold on auction blocks in broad daylight because it's a legal, normal American business trade. Blacks could still be legally declared only three-fifths human. Jim Crow laws could still be on the books and people would still have to use separate water fountains, bathrooms; or we could still be riding on segregated buses, etc. This is all true. Many things have changed. But the most important thing has not: There is still not human equality in America.

All citizens are not being treated as if they are created equal. Have you looked at the best seller lists lately? The American publishing industry screams this from the top of these lists everyday. It is an undeniable fact. So none of us, black, white, blue or green, can afford to be pacified by the progress that has been made up to now, and accept that as being enough. We must speak up and speak the truth until the subordinate treatment of certain Americans is completely eradicated.

The price and ramifications of racial divides are too high. This is why I am writing this book.

Chapter 8

IN CONCLUSION

My daughter Nadine is my one and only child. From the day she was born, I have loved her as much as any parent could love a child. I have always wanted the very best for her in her life. I tried to encourage her to become a lawyer, because I think she would make an excellent one, however, she chose to be a writer, and I am extremely proud of her choice and give her my full support.

As any parent can understand, seeing your child hurt is a devastating experience. What Penguin did to my daughter - by basically telling her she was born the wrong color if she wanted access to the stratosphere of the book business - has cut her to her core. I witnessed the pain she went through when she had to come to terms with them bringing the color of her skin into the publication of her books. And what they have done to her, they have done unto me also.

Now, unless you have been ill-treated in such a way, you may not be able to relate to how strongly this can cut a human being. My daughter even told me she considered taking her own life, but because of me and her mother she did not. She felt that death was better than third-class living. I think to this day she still believes that.

She discouraged me from writing this book, but I feel this information is too relevant to keep quiet. It is important to me to see more progress made toward equality in publishing, and for my daughter's struggles to have not been in vain. The discrimination against her books has crushed her spirit for writing, but I stay in hope that she will one day be able to find joy in writing once again.

I believe that Penguin Group gagged my daughter from ever speaking about what they did to her because they don't want the dirty laundry of their behavior exposed. I think it is vitally important to them, and to the other publishing giants, to maintain the appearance of being an equal opportunity publisher, while practicing something else entirely under the hood. But I ask you, the reader, to open your eyes. Preserve your own personal integrity. Look at the facts and the hard evidence. Published books and book covers don't lie. You must see the truth here and what it means for those who benefit from the present system...and also what it means for those who suffer from it.

This is a nationwide problem and the media needs to stop looking the other way when it comes to talking about the racial practices of today. Please think about this in an open and honest way and do what you can to support America's ideal and make our nation one that actually does provide freedom for all. We can do it together!

"We are out to defeat injustice and not white persons who may be unjust." - **Dr. Martin Luther King, Jr., STRIDE TOWARD FREEDOM (1964)**

ABOUT THE AUTHOR

Timothy Aldred is the father of author Millenia Black. His life is dedicated to the pursuit of justice and freedom for all. He lives in Florida.

He can be reached at http://www.timothyaldred.com